Diary of a Curvy Gal

By
Izzy Spears

"I have learned to live in the moment and love the body I have. Why wait for tomorrow?"

XOXO
Izzy Spears

Diary of a Curvy Gal

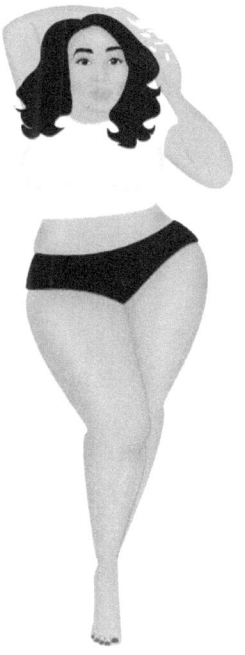

Izzy Spears

PaSH Publishing
Birmingham, Alabama

Published by PaSH Publishing

Copyright (c) 2018 by Izzy Spears

All Rights Reserved

Published in the United States by PaSH Publishing, an imprint of The Southern PaSH Company.
www.SouthernPash.com

PaSH Publishing and its logo are owned by The Southern PaSH Company.

Book cover illustration by Fashionlistically Speaking
Layout and cover design done by Kaneshia Sims Hudson

ISBN
978-0-9992852-2-0

Printed in the United States of America

First Edition

"Life is short. Dance like no one is watching, I do."

Izzy

"Life became so much easier once I started to say- F#$K the haters."

Izzy

Diary of a Curvy Gal

By
Izzy Spears

"I don't need permission to be myself."

Izzy

Table of Content

Chapter 1
Girl in the Mirror

Chapter 2
More Pain

Chapter 3
Finding Myself Again

Chapter 4
Loving Myself

Chapter 5
Dance Like No One is Watching

Chapter 6
The Constant Battle

"Why should I apologize for being myself?"

Izzy

about the author

Izzy Spears is a public relations and marketing professional, actress, model, author, entertainer and entrepreneur. She is founder of The Southern PaSH Company LLC, a public relations and consulting firm.

The Southern PaSH Company publishes a magazine, Red PaSH Magazine, and Izzy acts as editor-in-chief.

Before starting her career in the field of communications, Izzy made a name for herself as an interior decorator and home stager as owner of KanShe Staging.

As a reflection of her creative side, Izzy acted as head photographer and owner of KLS Photography for many years.

Izzy is a graduate of The University of Alabama at Birmingham and holds a B.A. in mass communications and a minor in psychology.

Additional skills Izzy brings to the table are public speaking, business coaching, photography and consulting.

Izzy started her journey as an actress and model after she decided she was going to learn how to put herself first. After vowing to no longer be crippled by fear, Izzy started her journey of living life out loud.

"Just because you are uncomfortable with my looks doesn't mean I have to be."

Izzy

chapter one

girl in the mirror

I can remember the first time I looked in the mirror and said to myself, "you aren't good enough." I was in the third grade. At that time, there was a cute boy that rode my school bus. I had the biggest crush on him. If memory serves me right, I was living in a small town. The town was so small everyone knew everyone. Knowing everyone was simple due to the fact that most people were related or most people were related to someone who was related to them. Yea, try and wrap your head around that. I vividly remember sitting on the school bus in silence. I would occupy my time by daydreaming about my little crush. I would look out the window and fantasize about the boy who held my eight year old heart.

The boy, whom will remain nameless, was smart, polite, courteous and in my opinion very attractive. Being young and naive, I thought my feelings were opaque. I had no clue that his cousin could see my infatuation with this boy. This cousin was the opposite of him in every single way. She was rude, loud, obnoxious and for reasons unknown to me; she could sense I had deep feelings for her cousin. Nevertheless, this did not sit well with her. She made it a point to taunt me daily. On Monday, she would pick at me about my hair style, on Tuesday, she would make fun of my outfit. The longer I sat on that bus in silence, not defending myself, the braver she became.

I was paralyzed by the embarrassment of her bullying. I felt small and helpless. Until THAT day.

On THAT day, she felt brave. I remember looking out the window as the bus driver pulled up to her house. I closed my eyes, praying she would not be present. I held my breath with anticipation. Could it be? Will I be spared? Will she be absent today? Of course not. The front door of her house sprung open and out ran my worse nightmare. I could see her red ribbons as she climbed the stairs to enter the bus. Our eyes meet. Before I could turn my head she blurted, "You're so fat, my cousin would never marry you." At that moment my heart stopped and my face turned red. Before I could utter a word, he came to my defense. Unfortunately, I don't remember his exact words, everything happened so quickly. I felt so many emotions at once. Part of me was pleased that he noticed me. In fact, I was speechless, I was in shock. I couldn't believe my crush had the guts to stand up to his bully of a cousin. I felt all this while the other part of me was hurt and very embarrassed.

Were the words she screamed for all to hear true? Was I too fat to marry? Did being fat mean I was ugly? Were her words valid? Was she just being mean? Did everyone else around me feel the way she felt? From that day on I avoided both him and her. Like I mentioned before, we lived in a small town. By the end of the day, everyone was whispering about me and my not so secret crush.

I knew he knew how I felt. I knew she knew she had broken me. My fantasy was over and a nightmare had begun.

"Who made them in charge of beauty standards? I like to set my own!"

Izzy

chapter two

more pain

As children, we typically float around day to day. We just exist. The world is bright and shinny and as long as we have our basic needs of food, water, shelter and clothing, our worlds are pretty small. As kids, we don't often think of others. Children don't understand the consequences of their actions and the harshness of their words. Then, all of a sudden, on one unpreventable day, the cloak of innocence is removed and everything is no longer as it once was.

I remember the day when the cloak of innocence was removed from my eyes. Yet again, I am getting off the school bus. By this time, my family has moved to a suburb outside the city of Atlanta, Georgia. We are living in an apartment complex. Everyday the bus driver drops clusters of children off in front of the leasing office. Everyday I mind my own business. I walk directly home, keeping to myself, not causing any trouble. For some reason unknown to me, I am the conversation topic of a small group of kids walking behind me. Suddenly, I hear a voice, "Your sister is FAT!" Immediately, my heart drops to the pit of my stomach. My instincts tell me to run and hide. Me still being the shy and timid kid that I was, I quickened my pace. I was attempting to run away from the embarrassment. I knew everything would be okay as long as I could get home. At home I am safe.

Over the next few days the same children continued to be cruel. "Why is she so fat?" they would yell into the air. "I can't believe she has to wear a bra.", others would shout. One day, I grew tired of remaining silent. I quickly turned to my sister, I stared into her eyes for support, I waited, but I received nothing from her. Suddenly, I felt anger. My body turned hot, my mind raced with emotions. I told myself, "Don't just walk away, don't let them win". The words "Your FAT" and "I don't care what YOU say!" rolled from my lips. Before I realized what had come over me, I pushed past the group and walked home alone.

That day, a tiny seed was planted inside me.

Later that night I approached my sister. I asked her

why she had not taken up for me. Her expression was blank and empty of concern. She stated, "What do you want me to do? You are fat."

At that moment, the second tiny seed was planted. The previous events taught me two things. One, the world is a mean and cruel place. Two, self-worth comes from within.

As the years progressed I become more and more aware of my body. I would do aerobic exercises in my room or walk at the track with my mother. At a very early age, I recall counting calories and drinking a gallon of water a day. At one point, asking God to make me thin was an addition to my nightly prayers.

During those dark moments of my life, I didn't like the way I looked. I gazed at my reflection in the mirror with discomfort. At that time I didn't know what type of body I wanted. All I knew is that mine was bad.

Puberty came early for me. I developed breasts in the third grade and my menstrual cycle came when I was in the fifth grade. Looking back at photos, I was not obese. I was simply a full figured girl. Compared to the girls my age, I looked like a teenager. Unfortunately for me, body positivity was not taught at home or in school. Finding clothing that fit my body was difficult. I wanted to dress like the other girls my age. I wanted to look like the other girls my age. These times were hard for me. I didn't have anyone I could talk to. I didn't have anyone who understood my pain.

    Fast forward to junior high school aka a complex war zone. There, boys, mean girls and the politics of being a teenager, start to blend together in one large soup. Being surrounded by the peer pressure to wear makeup, the latest threads and the coolest shoes is enough stress for the average teenage girl, let alone, a fat one.

One particular memory of junior high school sticks out vividly for me. I was at a basketball game. I was in the seventh grade at the time. The only reason I was attending a sporting event was due to the fact I was a member of student council. I had been assigned concession stand duty. I remember the music starting, signaling the beginning of halftime. Everyone rushed out to watch the dance team perform its routine. As the music played and the girls jumped, twirled and wowed the crowd, I thought to myself, I wish that could be me.

As I watched the girls, I never once thought, I, of all people, could be one of them. They were athletic, pretty and most of all, thin.

The half time show ended and I went to the restroom. I stood in the mirror, staring at my reflection. As I stood there, I reflected upon myself, my position at the school and the future I desired for myself.

I remember playing the song the dancers performed to in my head. I tried to picture my body dancing next to one of theirs. I looked at my reflection in the mirror and said to myself. Be realistic, you are a scholar. You belong on student council, not the dance team. At that very moment, a group of cheerleaders walked into the restroom. At first, I became intimidated. I offered a soft hello. Surprisingly, their responses were warm and friendly. Feeling brave, I said to one of the girls,"It looks like y'all are having a lot of fun?" She then said, "We are...you should try out. You would like it." She smiled then walked out of the restroom.

Little did that cheerleader know, that simple conversation changed my world forever. So many thoughts ran through my head. Could I actually make the dance team? Didn't she notice I am fat? If she didn't think I was fat, then maybe I have a chance. Maybe the judges won't care that I am fat either.

To prepare for tryouts I stretched and worked out at home. I was extremely excited to participate in tryouts. I had never done anything like trying out for a sports team before. Finally, the week of tryouts had arrived. Nothing could have prepared me for what was coming next.

Tryout week was full of drills, chants, routines and etiquette. We spent several hours learning a routine that would be performed in front of a panel of judges. Each day the gymnasium filled with girls of different sizes and skill sets. Prior to tryouts, I had never trained with a dance instructor a day in my life. Everything I was experiencing was brand new to me. Each day I did something new with my body that I had never done prior. To be honest, I did things I never knew I was capable of doing. Each morning I woke up so sore I could barely walk, but my determination out weighted the physical pain.

I remember both getting up early and staying up late to practice. I wanted nothing more than to see my name on the roster.

After five long days of preparing to tryout, I had no choice but to be ready. For the first time ever, I walked onto the basketball court ready to prove to the judges that I am worthy to be picked. I did exactly as I practiced. The judge called my name. I did my splits. I completed my turns. I smiled so hard my face was trembling. Now, it is time for the group routine. As music filled the gym, I could feel my heart race. At this point, there was no turning back. All I could do was wait for the cue. And just like that, within a blink of an eye, like an outer body experience, things happen. Your body takes over, you go blank. Then when it is all over, you are handed back the controls. Not sure of what happened or what the judges are thinking, I walk back to the holding room. Then, after what feels like ages, someone comes in and says, "the rosters are up." All the girls run to the wall where the names are posted. I wait for the room to clear. I take a deep breath and walk up to the wall. I can't believe my eyes. There it is, clear as day, my name. I must have been standing in that spot for a bit to long. One of the mothers came over to me and said congratulations. I said,"thank you", and shyly went to catch a ride home.

Being on that dance team made me fall in love with myself. The notion of someone falling in love with themselves may sound silly, but it is true. Up until that point, I didn't think I had any value. Falling in love with myself taught me I had worth, value and I was worth fighting for. I learned that no matter how my body looked I am worthy of whatever I put my mind to.

"A number on a scale does not define a person's value."

Izzy

chapter three

finding myself again

In college I was determined to be the opposite of who I was in high school. College was a clean slate and a new beginning. I didn't care for all the pressure I endured in high school. I didn't want to damper my college experience trying to be popular or fit in. In college I was just going to be me. I did not want to be in clubs, I did not want to play the popularity contest game and I definitely did not want to be a big cat on campus. I wanted the opportunity to find myself without the pressure of my peers.

Due to the injures I suffered to my knee in high school, I didn't try out for the dance team in college. Furthermore, I was burnt out academically. I just wanted to get a job and attend class like normal college students.

So, lets look at the facts. I am in college, freshmen 15 became freshmen 20. The cafeteria had all you could eat buffet in the eventing and my roommate and close friends ate all we could eat! We had fun chatting and tasting all the good food. Lets just say freshman 15 is real. I think freshmen 20 in my case. All in all, I was happy. I had gained a little weight but so what!? My friends weren't obsessed with being thin and I liked my new curvy body. It was fun being a little "thick".

My new body came with consequences. Shopping in the junior department became difficult. Due to my new curvy body, I was forced to shop in department stores outside of my comfort zone. Picking up garments in the misses section is when the reality of what happened to my body sunk in. I could not just pick up a pair of pants or a blouse and know it would fit. The days of having a lean and trim body were over. At that point I knew I needed an intervention.

The task of dressing my new body affected my confidence. Mostly because I did not know were to shop. Then and there I made a promise to "fix" what I had done to myself. I started working out every night and counting my calories. I was slowly becoming the constricted individual I was before. Noticeably, something was missing. My desire to get in shape was present but I lacked the other factors that fueled the fire that had long ago burned out. I no longer had the motivation of being a dancer. The long practices I participated in were now replaced with long shifts at work. My days are now filled with class and studying. My life was different. I was no longer an athlete. I had to find a way to love my new body and maintain a healthier lifestyle.

> "Telling yourself you will begin to live life once you reach a fitness goal is sabotage."
> Izzy

chapter four

loving myself

Daily I am reminded about how "fat" I am. I watch television and I see very few people that look like me. I sit in a chair in a waiting room and I fill it completely. I ride in a plane and the aisles and seats are too tiny for my frame. The reminder of my body is always present. I can honestly say I don't remember when I made the discussion to love my body. All I can remember is making the discussion not to hate my body. A person can spend all his or her days trying to become the perfect version of themselves. Wasting valuable time before they truly start living.

chapter five

dance like no one is watching

Society tells me I am a plus size girl. The clothes I buy are usually 16-18 in dresses and XL in blouses; yet I wear what I want. Thanks to Stacy and Clinton from TLC's "What Not to Wear", I have learned you have to dress for your body; and all bodies are different. Guess what, that is okay.

When I walk into a room, I don't feel intimidated, I stand tall and feel confident. I feel sexy, pretty and comfortable in my own skin. Yes, there are days when I look in the mirror and pull and tug. As a female, I think we all do. But, overall, I love myself.

I have learned that you are who you are and you also have the power to make small modifications to your appearance. You can color your hair, polish your nails or wear high heals. You can also change your appearance drastically with plastic surgery, stuffing your bra or wearing constraining garments such as corsets. If you choose to do so, that is your personal choice.

I am confident that loving yourself comes from self-worth. That no matter your size, how tall you are or how much you weigh, you must believe you have value as a person.

I have always struggled with maintaining my weight. I go up and down and fluctuate quite often. At my lowest weight, I was a dancer on my high school dance team. I love to dance. Although I don't dance professionally, dance is still a huge part of my life. With four hour practices and my own work out routine at home, exercise was a big part of my life back in high school. In hindsight I was thin, but at the time, I still felt large next to my other team mates. I worked extra hard to gain strength and stay in shape. I enjoyed my athletic body, running and lifting weights felt good. Running two miles a day was nothing for me. Going to the track and walking 10 miles a day was normal. That life style is not realistic for me today. As a result, I don't have the same "skin" as I did then. Today I still enjoy going to the gym. I hope to work toward my black belt in Tae-Kwon-Do soon. Just because you change on the outside doesn't mean you are a different person on the inside.

Today I am a plus size gal that in her past was what society now defines as average. I still wear my short skirts, high heals and at times, the necessary cleavage. I am not afraid of bodycon dresses and wearing my sleeveless tops. Yes, I might be a little fluffy, but I love myself. And most importantly, I always dance like no one is watching.

Life is too short for regrets.

> "Setting around waiting for someone to validate your existence is like dying of thirst while a spring of fresh water bubbles within arms reach."

Izzy

chapter six

the constant battle

When you are a plus size person, it can be hard to look into the mirror. Staring into the mirror is difficult, not because you don't love yourself, but because the media, society and those around you, can make it hard for you to like yourself. All day we are force-fed images of thin, youthful individuals. These individuals are slim, have flawless hair, flawless makeup and the best wardrobe. But, as many of us know, this is not a true reflection of all the women of society. Where are the individuals that look like us?

Due to the lack of a representation of individuals

that look like us (curvy, lumpy and not straight up and down) we subconsciously dislike our appearance. Daily, we find ourselves spending time on beauty rituals. We create bad spending habits on waste trainers, diet pills, body shapers and cosmetic surgery to reflect what we see around us. All the while, slowly disliking who we are, hating the body we have and striving to be something we are not.

As a professional, who occasionally appears on television, whose image is constantly captured and who speaks in front of crowds filled with eyes gazing at me, I can honestly say, being in front of a camera can be intimidating. Sure, it is typical to wonder if you have food in your teeth or if your blouse is undone. As a curvy gal, the intimidating part is walking into the room with my head held high as people gaze. Some people stare with a look of astonishment. They ask themselves, why is she so confident? I know because plenty of women approach me and say things like, "I could never wear a skirt, my legs are way too large". Or they say, "I could never wear a dress that form fitting, but you look nice."

I feel as if some people feel larger people should walk around shoulders slumped and eyes to the ground. It is my opinion that people feel curvy gals don't deserve to be noticed or deserve to have a place in the world. I have noticed that people feel uncomfortable with how comfortable I am in my own skin. What? Am I suppose to go around hoping not to be noticed? Am I suppose to be an invisible object fading into the background? Why is it taboo for me to love myself, love fashion and wear high heals (looking flawless I might add) regardless of my dress size?

I want curvy gals to love their bodies. I want to inspire others. I want other gals to say, if she can love herself, if she can feel comfortable in her skin, then so can I!

Sometimes I run across other curvy gals that are inspired and they ask where I shop or how I have the courage to dress so freely? My response is always the same. I always say, "love yourself and flaunt it if you got it. You only live once."

Okay, now that I am done with that rant, I want to be honest. I am not going to say that I have never asked my husband the typical, "how do I look", because I do. I am human.

The purpose of sharing my story is to declare I have learned to love myself, body included.

I may never be the 160 pounds I was as a teen. I am okay with that.

I have learned how to dress for my body type. Which makes a world of difference I might add. And, I have learned how to dress for the occasion. Feeling good about yourself while being comfortable in your own skin is a daily battle for a lot of people. For me, this battle begins every morning when I step into my closet.

There are times when I look into the mirror and I don't like what I see. I may have gained a little weight or my breasts are a little fuller. I don't get depressed or disgusted. Instead, I am empowered by the fact that I can make simple adjustments in my life to see the desired changes to my body, or not.

Please don't get me wrong. I am not being hyper-critical by saying I watch what I eat and exercise to maintain my personal desired weight, because I do. That is a personal choice. Although watching what I eat and exercising still has not granted me a dress size that is considered a social norm; staying active keeps me healthy and reduces my stress. I realize that I am not okay with body shaming and making people feel bad about themselves. I am not saying people can't strive to reach personal goals in health and fitness. I am saying don't judge others because their goal is not similar to yours.

One day I may wake up and say, I want a six pack. I would begin the journey down the road taking the necessary steps to achieve that particular goal. But, never should that be the social standard of beauty.

This is a wonderful time to be alive. Technology has made it possible for people across the world to share their stories. Love yourself for who you are today. Don't wait for tomorrow. Girl Power!

"My weight was the topic of many conversations. Why does society place such an emphasis on something that is not its business?"

Izzy

"Body shaming is not okay. No one has the right to minimize anyone."

Izzy

"I have learned that confidence is a lethal weapon."

Izzy

acknowledgments

It is such a blessing to be able to share this book with everyone. I want to take a moment and thank my husband, Warren. He is such an amazing man. He is a great friend and amazing lover.

I also want to thank my son. The glow of his eyes light the path of my future. The two of them motivate me to strive for the best and reach for the stars.

I love you both,

Izzy

"I dedicate this book to all the little girls. You are pretty. You are beautiful. You are special. You are enough. You are perfect just the way you are."

Izzy

more about me

I am excited to offer the following bonus pages. I have shared bits of my past. Now, I want to share bits of my present. The next few pages will have tips on how I learned to love myself, live out loud and put my best foot forward, all in attempts to be the best version of myself possible.

 I thank you for reading my book. It means the world to me. Check out www.izzyspears.com to stay up to date with what I am up to.

xoxo,

Izzy

photo credit: Samantha Sheldon

thank you for capturing my true essence.

twelve ways Izzy lives better

1. I drink plenty of water

2. I make time to eat real food

3. I listen to my body

4. I learned how to say no

5. I started saying f#$% the haters

6. I stopped asking for permission

7. I started trusting my gut

8. I stopped wearing high heels

9. I stopped apologizing

10. I wear what I want

11. I wear my natural hair

12. I take naps

twelve ways I will live better

ten ways Izzy lives out loud

1. I wear red lipstick
2. I wear crop tops just because I can
3. I only wear the color black
4. I dance when ever and where ever I hear music
5. I drink plenty of coffee
6. I believe in utilizing every moment I can for PDA (public displays of affection) with my husband.
7. I speak my mind
8. I ask plenty of questions
9. My motto is "why not?"
10. I always remember tomorrow is not promised

ten ways I will live out loud

ten ways Izzy loves herself

1. I carve out at least 30 minutes a day for some "me time"
2. I keep a journal of all my goals and aspirations.
3. I look in the mirror each morning, smile and say, "I am beautiful"
4. I make a point to always do something I have never done before
5. I get rid of everything that is negative in my life
6. I throw away all clothing that does not fit
7. I allow myself to make mistakes
8. I tell myself I am worthy of happiness
9. I embrace my imperfections
10. I eat chocolate

ten ways I will love myself

_____
_____
_____
_____
_____
_____
_____
_____
_____
_____
_____
_____
_____
_____

reasons I wrote this book

I have lived the majority of my life being judged for my appearance. I was constantly bullied at school for my appearance and my weight. Family members often felt comfortable judging me about my weight and making jokes about how I looked. These events hurt me emotionally and psychologically. I spent many hours exercising, counting calories and wishing I looked like someone else. No one ever wrapped their arms around me and told me I was beautiful. No one ever said it is okay to be different. I am sharing a few pages from my diary to let other people know that they are not alone.

There is no reason to suffer in silence. Bullying is not okay. Teasing someone because they look different should not be tolerated in our society.

People of different shapes and sizes as well as physical and mental abilities are all deserving of love and acceptance. I am sharing key moments of my life that have scared me, shaped me or transformed me into the person I am today.

I can say with pride that I love myself. I don't care to hear what others have to say about my clothing, my hair, my size or my lifestyle. I hope the words in this book can help you find the strength to do the same.

xoxo

Izzy

This Book Belongs To:

Please Return To:

Contact Info:

www.ingramcontent.com/pod-product-compliance
Lightning Source LLC
Chambersburg PA
CBHW030458010526
44118CB00011B/993